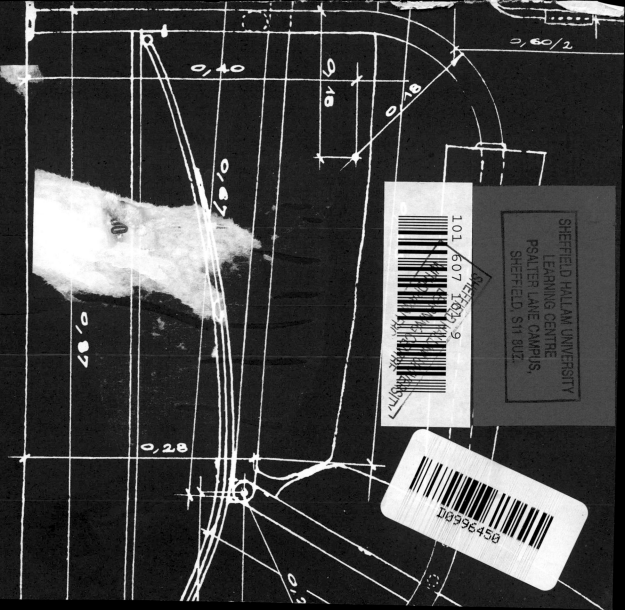

THE
CHAIR

THE

CHAIR

AN APPRECIATION

AURUM PRESS

SARAH COLOMBO ☉ PHOTOGRAPHS BY GUY RYECART

First published in Great Britain 1997 by
Aurum Press Limited, 25 Bedford Avenue,
London WC1B 2AT

A catalogue record for this book
is available from the British Library

ISBN 1 85410 526 4

This book was conceived,
designed and produced by
THE IVY PRESS LIMITED
2/3 St Andrews Place, Lewes,
East Sussex BN7 1UP

Art Director: *Peter Bridgewater*
Commissioning Editor: *Viv Croot*
Managing Editor: *Anne Townley*
Editors: *Graham Smith, Julie Whitaker*
Page layout: *Ron Bryant-Funnell*
Photography: *Guy Ryecart*

Printed and bound in China

Throughout this book the specification for the material
of manufacture of each chair is given with the frame
material first followed by the seat material.
Dimensions are given in imperial and metric
measurements; height, width, and depth and
expressed by H, W and D.

22

15

12

23

29

25

25

20

11

20

15

24

30

12

26

22

16

21

21

19

14

10

31

23

17

19

10

18

11

28

27

26

14

31

13

28

Introduction

Throughout history the chair has been designed as a symbol of hierarchy and of power relationships in public life. From the opulent regal throne to the humble wooden stool, these most functional of objects have a social significance beyond their mere appearance. The 20th century has seen two fundamental influences on the form of the chair – firstly, the growth of the architect as proto-designer, and secondly, the merging of design with problem solving – with the end result that design has become art.

Many classic chairs of the 20th century were designed by architects as extensions of their broader

Eero Arnio
Pastilli Chair, 1968

Michael Thonet
#14 Chair, 1959

architectural theories, as in the work of Mies van der Rohe. The collection in this book also highlights the use of chair design to develop the theories of volume, speed and structure founded in art movements. Designs such as Gerrit Rietvelt's Red Blue and Zig-Zag Chairs illustrate the definition of space already explored in the works of artists such as Dutch painter Piet Mondrian.

Ludwig Mies van der Rohe
MR 20/3 Chair, 1929

The Modernists of the early 20th century attempted to dictate the total form of the domestic environment and, in the process, to stamp their ideologies of design, and indeed living, upon the urban populations of Europe, the USA and beyond. An integral part of the Modern design ideology was the role of the architect as the great designer of life, uniquely qualified by virtue of training and education to regulate our space for the common good. However, as the tower blocks and offices of the 1960s began to crash down around the startled ears of their inhabitants, the notion of an

Danny Lane
Etruscan Chair, 1984

Arne Jacobsen
No. 3317 Aegget
'Egg Chair', 1958

all-knowing designer lost much of its viability as a cultural *Zeitgeist*.

Chairs became soft, and moulded to the body's natural shape as foam padding accommodated the curves and bulges of nature. Whimsy and the colours of the nursery overtook the monochrome, rectilinear spaces of earlier days. In the late 20th century, the resurgence of craft values blurred the lines between gallery art and design for production, in the work of artist-designer-makers such as Tom Dixon and Ron Arad. This move away from factory production, and the corresponding shift from a functional aesthetic to the aesthetic of wonder and glorious impracticability, represents a serious challenge to Modernism and its plea for rational objectivity.

Throughout the 20th century we can see in the iconic chairs of each period a symbol of the larger social and economic changes in the industrialized world. Modernism is enthralled with industrial production,

Michele De Lucchi
First, 1983

and holds that the design of domestic life should reflect the right-angles and rigidity of the machine. At the other extreme, Post-Modernism indulges in a self-conscious plunder of history as it endlessly pillages the past. Marcel Breuer's Wassily Chair of 1925 and Danny Lane's

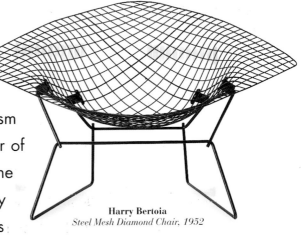

Harry Bertoia
Steel Mesh Diamond Chair, 1952

Etruscan Chair of 1984 perfectly reflect these polar opposites.

Some of the chairs shown here acquired fame through the revolutionary application of new materials, most noticeably in the organic, moulded forms of fibreglass explored by Eero Arnio in his Ball Chair of 1965 and in the heat-sealing techniques that made possible the inflatable Blow Chair designed two years later by the team of Scolari, d'Urbino, Lomazzi and de Pas.

This collection represents only a small proportion of the fascinating, and at times outrageous, chairs produced in the course of the 20th century, and reflects the energy and creativity of one of the most inventive and exciting design periods.

GERRIT RIETVELT
RED BLUE CHAIR

TUBULAR STEEL/OILCLOTH, 1925,
H28.75 X W30.75 X D27.5IN
H73 X W78 X D70CM

Based on an invisible structure of intersecting lines that delineate volume, Rietvelt's black-framed chair draws clear parallels between art, design and architecture. Designed to stand against a black wall, as in its present position in the Schröder-Schräder house in the Netherlands, its coloured sections give the appearance of floating in space.

WOOD, 1917-18,
H34.25 X W26 X D32.75IN
H87 X W66 X D83.5CM

MARCEL BREUER
WASSILY CHAIR

This gravity-defying chair seems to hover on the surface of the floor. Straps and tubes, solidity and space, work on the eye, drawing us into the black rectangular obelisk. Designed for Wassily Kandinsky, the chair's capacity to dazzle is as strong today as it was in the 1920s. Strong and light, the Wassily cocoons the sitter in its powerful, low and deep seat.

MART STAM
CHAIR S 33

Compared with Mies van der Rohe's MR chair of the same time, Stam's S 33 appears utilitarian and lacking in style. Yet, fitted with canvas and leather seating, it has inspired a thousand imitations, effortlessly spanning the boardroom, laboratory, hospital and school. Design students still scavenge building sites for examples, in search of its obsessive simplicity.

LUDWIG MIES VAN DER ROHE
MR 20/3 CHAIR

Mies van der Rohe's passion for clean Modern lines and the functional aesthetic influenced many European and US designers, and his work represents a high point for the architects' domination of chair design. The cantilever principle is the most eye-catching feature of the MR chairs, which came both with and without tubular steel armrests. The cane seating panel was reproduced at a later date in leather.

TUBULAR STEEL/CANE & LEATHER, 1929, H32.75 X W18.25 X D26.75IN / H83.5 X W46.5 X D68CM

STEEL/LEATHER, 1929,
H29.5 X W29.5 X D29.5IN
H75 X W75 X D75CM

LUDWIG MIES VAN DER ROHE
BARCELONA CHAIR

This large classic chair takes its name from the International Exhibition of 1929 and was specifically designed for the interior of the German Pavilion. Reproductions have since graced the foyers and receptions of many multinational corporations. Its simple, sweeping lines and opulent materials have ensured the chair a place in design history beyond the confines of Modernism.

GERRIT RIETVELT
ZIG-ZAG CHAIR

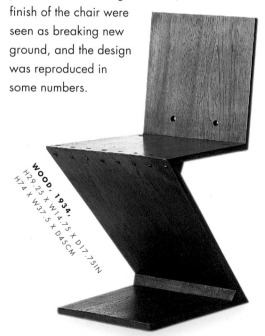

Rietvelt intended this chair as an essential part of a total environment, as in the Schröder-Schräder house, in which the chair has a role in delineating space and, to that end, occupies as little volume as possible. The primitive cantilevering and stark, unadorned finish of the chair were seen as breaking new ground, and the design was reproduced in some numbers.

WOOD, 1934,
H29.25 X W14.75 X D17.75IN
H74 X W37.5 X D45CM

TUBULAR STEEL/CANVAS, 1938,

H34.75 X W22.75 X D23.5IN

H88 X W58 X D60CM

J. F. HARDOY, A. BONET & J. KURCHEN

HARDOY

Abreathtakingly simple chair in a surprisingly free-form frame of bent metal, this design prefigures so much of the following 30 or 40 years in chair design. The seemingly random design of the metal leg carefully balances confidence and strength with the greatest feeling for space.

STEEL/FIBREGLASS, 1949, H32.25 X W25.25 X D24IN / H82 X W64 X D61CM

WOOD/LEATHER, 1949,
H28.5 X W22 X D20.5IN
H72.5 X W56 X D52CM

CHARLES EAMES

DAR CHAIR

The design of this chair was a collaborative response by Charles Ray Eames and a number of colleagues from the engineering department at the University of California to a low-cost furniture competition set by the Museum of Modern Art in 1948. The moulded seat was the first to use fibreglass, and the chair came in a limited range of colours.

HANS J. WEGNER

JH501 'THE CHAIR'

Dubbed 'The Chair' by journalists at its unveiling, Wegner's chair was immediately recognized as a timeless classic. The beautiful attention to detail and lavish hand finishing on the chair are testament to Wegner's rigorous apprenticeship in the Scandinavian workshops, and to his fascination with the surface and form of his native woods.

ERNEST RACE

ANTELOPE CHAIR

Designed for the 1951 British Festival of Britain, the Antelope Chair is the epitome of 'Festival style', with its multicoloured, wiry design. Exhibited outdoors on the terraces of the South Bank exhibition site in London, the chair was specifically constructed to withstand the rigours of the English weather. Offered in a choice of six colours, the Antelope won the Silver Medal at the Milan Triennale of 1954.

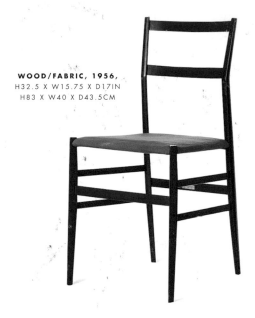

WOOD/FABRIC, 1956,
H32.5 X W15.75 X D17IN
H83 X W40 X D43.5CM

STEEL/PLYWOOD, 1950,
H31 X W22 X D22.5IN
H79 X W56 X D57CM

GIO PONTI

699 SUPERLEGGERA

This super-light chair, with its wafer-thin seat and tapered legs of delicate ash wood or stained walnut, lives up to its name and provides a spare model for those with spartan tastes. First and foremost an architect, Ponti considers all design to be an extension of architecture: 'I am an architect. I am not interested in the fashionable novelty...'

STEEL MESH, 1952, H30 X W21.25 X D21IN / H76 X W54 X D53CM

HARRY BERTOIA
STEEL MESH DIAMOND CHAIR

Bertoia was first employed by the Knoll company in his capacity as a trained sculptor, to experiment with the form of the chair, and his design shows a deep interest in the effects of space and volume. The use of steel mesh (strong enough to support without distortion, yet with a sufficiently wide weave to allow the maximum amount of light) marks this chair out as an exceptional and ground-breaking design.

CHARLES EAMES

LOUNGE CHAIR 670
& OTTOMAN 671

This masculine lounge chair illustrates beautifully the merging of office and home design that prevailed in American furniture design in the late 1950s. The essential supported softness and reclining swivel are married with a dark leather finish reminiscent of the boardroom. This chair sits alone as a design classic, but is also indicative of the increased crossover between work and leisure.

PLYWOOD, ALUMINIUM/LEATHER, 1956,
CHAIR:
H32.25 X W33 X D34.5IN
H82 X W84 X D87.5CM,

OTTOMAN:
H17.25 X W25.5 X D20.75IN
H44 X W65 X D53CM

EERO SAARINEN

TULIP PEDESTAL CHAIR

The organic aura of this tulip pedestal chair resembles much of the early 1960s' moulded concrete architecture and plastic futuristic designs, in which the only remaining organic forms are those featured in human-crafted works. Although the chair appears a unified whole, the pedestal is made from aluminium and the seat from a fibreglass shell.

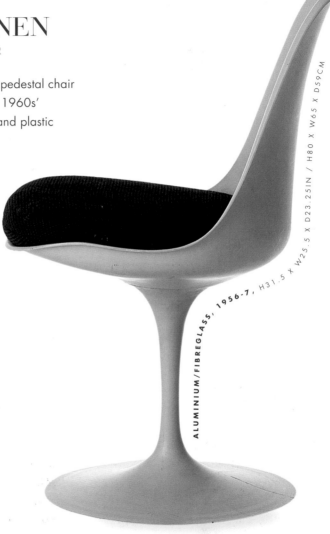

ALUMINIUM/FIBREGLASS, 1956-7, H31.5 X W25.5 X D23.25IN / H80 X W65 X D59CM

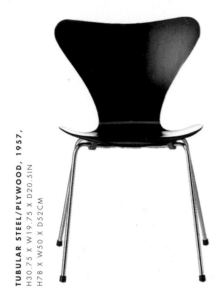

TUBULAR STEEL/PLYWOOD, 1957,
H30.75 X W19.75 X D20.5IN
H78 X W50 X D52CM

ALUMINIUM, FIBREGLASS/FOAM, 1958,
H34 X W42 X D31IN / H86 X W107 X D81CM

ARNE JACOBSEN

3107 CHAIR

Elegant, biomorphic forms characterize Jacobsen's chair designs, and nowhere more so than in this famous and widely copied chair. In recent years, coloured versions have come to grace many smart cafés and offices. The clean lines echo the female form, and it has the light, airy appearance of late 1950s' chair design throughout Europe and America.

ARNE JACOBSEN

NO. 3317 AEGGET
'EGG CHAIR'

Jacobsen's experiments in organic form are seen in this chair. He uses a moulded fibreglass shell with foam upholstery to create a smooth, womb-like cup on an aluminium base. The projecting horns are redolent of skin stretched taut over bone, and indeed the chair covering can sag and wrinkle over time.

FIBREGLASS, 1960, H32.25 X W19.25 X D22.5IN / H82 X W49 X D57CM

WOOD, STEEL/OXHIDE, 1961, H33.5 X W34.25 X D34.75IN H85 X W87 X D88CM

VERNER PANTON

RED CHAIR

Panton's Red Chair is a classic piece of moulded design that shouts the capacities of the new moulded fibreglass with a joyful red swagger. It is fluid and glossy, in the style of a car body and with a counter-balancing base that saves the seat back from banality. This stacking chair is a pure expression of material form.

HANS J. WEGNER

EASY CHAIR

Built on a wooden frame, with chromium-plated steel pipes, this piece is probably Wegner's favourite comfy chair. It dominates any room with its space-age sweeping legs and projecting headband. Also known as the Ox Chair, it has an oxhide covering and projecting horns at the top edges of the head rest.

EERO ARNIO

BALL CHAIR

PLASTIC, 1966–7,
H23.25 X W21.75 X D26.5IN / H59 X W55 X D67CM

A familiar sight in magazines of the 1960s, this chair is a natural candidate for iconic status. With a pedestal base reminiscent of Saarinen's Tulip Chair, the pod is a continuation of the sculptural experiments of Henry Moore and Barbara Hepworth, revealing the period's fascination with cellular forms and with a future in which technology might imitate nature.

LIISI BECKMANN

KARELIA

The late 1960s saw a marked increase in foam-padded soft furnishing and a turning away from the architectural principles governing much furniture design. It is precisely the throwaway nature of this piece – a curling, upturned caterpillar in the shining red plastic that was *de rigueur* – that gives it its importance.

GLASS REINFORCED POLYESTER, STEEL/FABRIC, 1965,
H43.25 X W38.25 X D33.75IN
H110 X W97 X D86CM

PVC, 1967,
H33 X W47.25 X D39.5IN
H84 X W120 X D100CM

SCOLARI, D'URBINO, LOMAZZI & DE PAS

BLOW CHAIR

A zany concept, the style of the Blow Chair perfectly captures the spirit of Italian design in the late 1960s, uniting new technology with glorious impracticability. Surprisingly resilient, the PVC was sealed by radio waves. Mass produced in four colours, these chairs combined an interesting design with the necessity of meeting the demands of an expanding consumer market.

EERO ARNIO

PASTILLI CHAIR

The rounded undercarriage of this moulded fibreglass shell makes this chair appear to float above the floor. Industrial/interior designer Arnio moved radically from Scandinavian contemporary design to embrace the biomorphic plasticity that new production processes unleashed from the late 1950s onwards. The chair's smooth finish and pod-like form link it to the work of contemporary sculptors as did Arnio's earlier Ball Chair.

FIBREGLASS, 1968,
H20.5 X W35.5 X D35.5IN / H52 X W90 X D90CM

STUDIO 65
BOCCA

A slightly reworked version of Salvador Dali's Mae West's Lips Wall Seat (c.1936), Bocca's fantasy objectification of body parts is made real in this pouting homage to sexually charged, dominant womanhood. The reworking of this art piece is homage indeed to its iconic status, and the reference to Surrealism within the context of pop design makes this work doubly interesting.

POLYURETHANE FOAM/FABRIC, 1970, H33.75 X W71.5 X D31.5IN / H86 X W182 X D80CM

TUBULAR STEEL, POLYSTYRENE/VINYL, 1970, H28 X W24.25 X D28.75IN H71 X W62 X D73CM

ACHILLE CASTIGLIONI
PRIMATE

A dual-function design that combines the cantilevered stool with a full seat. Viewed from a second angle, the chair takes on the appearance of an oversized coffee cup with a foaming cappucino top. The dark bottom portion of the chair adds lightness to what is a remarkably solid piece.

GRUPPO
DAM LIBRO

This chair epitomizes the move from the severity of Modernism, with its appeal to logic and the machine, to the pop aesthetic of the 1960s, which challenged the architectural emphasis in furniture design. Libro expresses the fascination with soft furnishing forms that dominated chair and sofa design in the 1970s and led to the free-form beanbag and the more structured modular form.

ALUMINIUM, FOAM RUBBER/ PLASTIC, 1970,
H29 X W22 X D19.75IN / H74 X W56 X D50CM

POLYURETHANE, 1971,
H31 X W20.5 X D32.25IN / H79 X W52 X D82CM

STUDIO 65
CAPITELLO

The Studio 65 designers pointed an early and prophetic finger towards the late 1980s with this visual pun on the aesthetics of classicism. The iconic status of the architectural column is made wonderfully trivial and thrusts through the living-room floor from a visual culture that, although retaining a strong design presence, is here largely emasculated by a teasing new upstart.

ETTORE SOTTSASS JUNIOR
Z9/R SEDIA DATTILO

Much envied and copied, this roller-based adjustable office chair marries concern for ergonomic design with the colours and fabric of the domestic environment. It proved a powerful combination, setting a new standard for comfort in design and challenging the common assumption that office furniture should be monochromatic.

ALUMINIUM, PLASTIC/FABRIC, 1972,
H33.25 X W19.25 X D19.25IN
H84.5 X W49 X D49CM

MICHELE DE LUCCHI

FIRST

First was designed under the auspices of the Italian design group Memphis, whose loose affiliation of designers included Ettore Sottsass. The group revolutionized furniture design in the late 1970s and early 1980s. Labelled Post-Modernism, the key indicators of the movement are the use of bright or 'feminine' colours and geometric volumes perched upon the tubes so favoured by Modernist designers such as Mies van der Rohe.

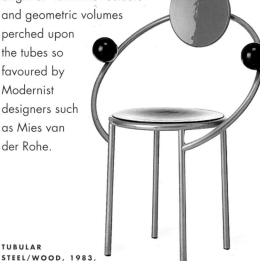

TUBULAR STEEL/WOOD, 1983,
H28.25 X W23.5 X D18.75IN
H72 X W60 X D48CM

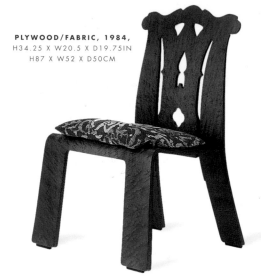

PLYWOOD/FABRIC, 1984,
H34.25 X W20.5 X D19.75IN
H87 X W52 X D50CM

ROBERT VENTURI

QUEEN ANNE

This complex chair makes a pastiche of the Queen Anne style with its cut-back rest and references to the plywood experiments of the 1930s. Venturi, at his zenith in the early 1980s, epitomized the jokey, ironic approach of the Italian Post-Modernist designers, and this chair carries an almost anthropomorphic aura, as do the best designs of Post-Modern furniture.

DANNY LANE

ETRUSCAN CHAIR

The antithesis of the mass-produced object, Lane's chair keeps its feet firmly in the arena of fine art, both in its name and its construction, thereby fulfilling the craft aesthetic of the late 1980s. Yet its functional nature fulfils the Modernist perception of the designer working for an industrial client, and challenges our perception of comfort necessarily being in opposition to art.

STEEL/GLASS, 1984,
H32.35 X W21.75 X D22IN
H82 X W55 X D56CM

TOM DIXON
S CHAIR

CARDBOARD, 1986,
H30 X W25.5 X D22IN
H76 X W65 X D56CM

The S Chair is formed in a sculptural process with little drawing or 'designing' work, as Dixon prefers to build each piece of furniture up from scratch, often incorporating pieces of recycled metal and manufactured objects. With its metal 'feet' positioned at a load-bearing angle, the chair invites the sitter to trust in its strength and comfort, regardless of its slim line and light appearance.

FRANK GEHRY
CARDBOARD CHAIR 'LITTLE BEAVER'

In a post-industrial world, the detritus of consumption slides across the cultural floor and crash-lands in the gallery. Gehry plays with the discarded packaging of the late 20th century within the form of an overstuffed popular Modernism of the 1930s, just as he plays with the knowing historicism of late 1980s' design.

STEEL/RUSH, 1985,
H43.25 X W21.75 X D20.5IN
H110 X W55 X D52CM

PHILIPPE STARCK

GOD RAYSSE

The more you look at this stool, the more its form changes from animal leg and buttock to street light, to serpent's head. Its opaque square base serves to emphasize the gravity-defying form of the design and the aluminium finish is reminiscent of aircraft design, a popular theme for bar and restaurant interiors in the late 1980s.

STEEL, 1987, H32.35 X W17.75 X D16.5IN / H82 X W45 X D42CM

STEEL, 1988,
H28.25 X W26.75 X D22.75IN
H72 X W68 X D58CM

RON ARAD

BIG EASY VOL. 2

Working around the post-punk movement, Arad emphatically rejected the mass-production ethos while embracing materials traditionally associated with heavy industry. By using welded metal in traditional domestic interior design, Arad imposed a stark contradiction between raw materials and the plump armchair aesthetic.

ALUMINIUM,
POLYURETHANE/PLASTIC, 1990,
H33.75 X W20.5 X D32.25IN
H86 X W52 X D82CM

ALDO ROSSI

PARIGI

This design is representative of the severe interpretation of Post-Modernism that characterizes much of Rossi's work. The surface patterning, so beloved of Post-Modern designs, is replaced here by block colour. Drama is provided by the swept, backward-leaning frame. The burnished metal, tube-like armrests race down to form legs that leave the sitter with the unsettling feeling of being in a wind tunnel.

PHILIPPE STARCK

LOUIS 20

In this design, a classically simple chair form is strikingly subverted in solid block colour and a slim metal finish. Starck has achieved world renown for his chair designs, and in the Louis 20 he has created a chair that combines the wit of Post-Modern pastiche with the severity of Modernism.

ALUMINIUM/
POLYPROPYLENE 1992,
H33.5 X W19 X D19.25IN
H85 X W48.5 X D49CM

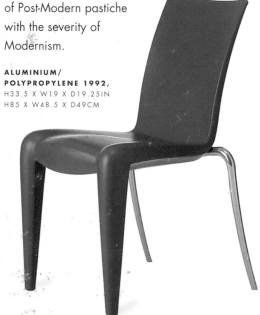

ACKNOWLEDGMENTS

The publishers would like to thank **The Vitra Design Museum**, Weil-am-Rhein, Germany for its invaluable help with photography.

Endpapers: Working drawing courtesy of the British Architectural Library, RIBA, London

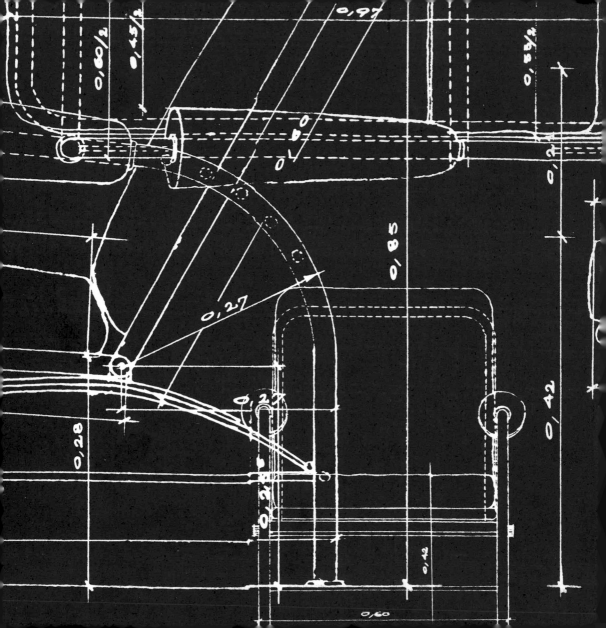